To Elspeth

with best wishes

Barry Cren

A Privilege and a Pleasure

A Life with Flowers

Barry Grey

This book is one of a special edition of 1500

To
Jill, Pat and Christopher
my team of three
with my love

Without your tremendous
support, in so many
ways, this book
would not have
been possible

Always there for
me and asking nothing
in return

Foreword by

Jill Grayston

Indeed, it is a privilege and a pleasure to write the Foreword for this beautiful book which illustrates so well the life and warmth of character of its author. Whilst Barry Grey's love of flowers is inherited and nurtured from gardening with his mother, his adult life within the world of flower arranging began in the 1970's when he trained at the London School of Floristry.

An exemplary floral artist whose work is known and admired at home and abroad through his demonstrations and teaching, Barry was also chief designer for the Millennium Flower Festival in Chester Cathedral. This talented artist is, furthermore, highly regarded for his poetry, inspired by his love of the beauty of nature. Today, much of Barry's time is occupied with his popular School of Floral Art and Design based on the Fylde Coast.

Barry's love of nature, and of people, coupled with his talent for art and creative pursuits and with a flower arranger's proverbial 'seeing eye', particularly shown in his glorious colour combinations, have all been brought together within the pages of this delightful book. His stunning designs are beautifully captured by prize-winning photographer David Lloyd whose images bring to life in sharp relief the immaculate plant material. The successful collaboration between two such artistic talents has given the reader a book to treasure but which also should be shared.

Destined to dig...

The demonstration outfits have changed over the years!

Can you hear me at the back of the hall?

A Privilege and a Pleasure

A life with flowers

So here it is, some will say "at last" - Barry's book. I do not seek to instruct or teach - that is for another place. If I inspire it is coincidental. Do not look too deeply for interpretation and meaning. It is purely for your enjoyment if, as I do, you like - nay love - flowers and foliage.

Over my 40 years of working with plant material I have seen many changes. Some to suit mood and fashion, others at the design of those who would seek to use plant materials as a means to a new art form. Minimalism, Modern, Abstract, Continental Plateau, Italian Mass, Structure work with twigs and sticks, Classic Period pieces - I cannot tell you how much I enjoy it all - indeed revel in it!

The plant materials which I can grow within our temperate climate - in , I might add, a very small overpacked, indeed jungleoid, garden - are a chief source of inspiration. But also plant materials we would only have glimpsed on an exotic holiday are now transported to our stockists within hours of being cut. We have world links through internet and publications which show us the way our fellow designers around the world arrange their flowers. Delving into these new, different and exciting styles and plant materials has been an extension of a fulfilled "English" background.

These pages, through fabulous flora and stunning photography, share with you my love of arranging. It has been a privileged career and I am conscious that brings with it a responsibility. My responsibility has been to share this - through stage, school, festival or workshop.

This book is the celebration of my life with flowers. It has not always been easy. Extensive hours, early mornings, late nights, nerves and frustrations are part of many careers - not least this one of mine. But to have worked with a material I love has been the joy, the motive, the impetus .....has been the privilege and the pleasure.

Barry Grey

Awakening to dawns first light
Another day of mottled sky
The shadows vanish, sun is bright
The night remembers times gone by

Float through the air as hazy dreams
Hues so subtle they mist away
Twisted glimpses from bygone scene
The visions flee with start of day

Brightest summer, coldest winter
Glare of sun and chill of snow
Life of spring with new birth hinted
Russet hue and candles glow

Dreaming memories of the seasons
Childhood, youth and then one's prime
No one told me, gave me reason
That all would pass, so swift the time

So here we stand and make our measure
Walk this earth, and place our mark
The gift, the art, the image treasure
As a new day dispels the dark

Fresh vistas mean we now move onward
Reality is clearing, dreams subside
We can go back but must go forward
Like waters edge at rise of tide

Grasping what each day does bring
Treading paths to light or shades
Fire will blaze and wind shall sing
No more to dream but action take
with purpose and resolve to make
our destiny before it fades

Barry Grey 2009

Awakening to dawn's
first light...

Hues so

subtle

they

mist

away

Brightest

summer

Gawsworth Hall
Cheshire

43

Coldest winter –

chill of snow

*Life of spring
with new birth hinted*

61

Russet hue and candle glow

The gift, the art
the image treasure

81

We can go back

but must go

forward

My grandmother

My parents on their wedding day

My grandfather

My grandparents

Like water's edge   at rise of tide

Walk this earth
and place our mark

Flower arranger at work

Photographer at rest

Bishop "Willy" of Gawsworth - ready for a wedding

Barry in action

Barry and cats

"I first started breeding Siamese in 1987 and so have had my prefix Flowerdew for 22 years. Some of the queens, layabouts and offspring are featured here.

As the feline family began to grow we had outside housing built to give some of the retired "ladies" a quieter life. I called in the electrician to make the necessary connections for the central heating system and lighting units. His account was addressed to "The Spoilt Flowerdew Siamese" and itemised; "To electrifying luxury cat apartments". Needless to say *they* did not pay the bill !!"

Acknowledgements

My thanks must be expressed to many people who have contributed to the production of this book.

Pat and John Bannister
Matt and Emma Brindley
Jill and David Hine
Timothy and Elizabeth Richards
All of whom have generously allowed me to use their
homes for photoshoots.

The Rector and congregation of Gawsworth Church for their
cooperation in staging the wedding flowers.

The Officers and Members of the Cheshire Area of NAFAS for help with
the Book Launch.

Mark Window of Manchester Wholesale Flowers for
continually sourcing beautiful plant material.

David Austin Flowers for the wonderful scented roses.

Lynn Breeze, Jill Connelly and Diane Fair for
the loan of containers.

Liz Beech - for chocolate cake and coffee
at exactly the right moments.

Annie Beagent - for her technical and administrative skills
throughout the production.

And finally to David Lloyd whose friendship, modest kindness, quiet manner and immense
talents has made this task yet another
privilege and pleasure.

First published by Spirit of the Rose Ltd
Lower Carterspiece Farm
English Bicknor
Near Coleford
Gloucestershire GL16 7ER
www.spiritoftherose.com

Photography © David Lloyd

The right of Barry Grey to be identified as the Author of the work has been asserted by him
in accordance with the Copyright, Designs and Patents Act 1988

A catalogue record of this book is available from the British Library
ISBN 978-0-9543939-6-0

Editors Barry Grey and Jill Grayston
Photographer David Lloyd
Scanning Design and Production
Annie Beagent (AB Imaging)
Printed by Hill Shorter